EASY PIZZA COOKBOOK

Step-By-Step Guide on How to Bake
Home-made Pizza Recipes at Home and For
Sale, Simple and Easy for Beginners

Christabel Henry

Table of Contents

Introduction

Welcome to the World of Home-made Pizza

Welcome to the savory universe of homemade pizza! In a world where culinary adventures abound, few dishes captivate taste buds and bring people together quite like pizza. This cookbook is an ode to the delightful art of creating pizzas from scratch, right in the heart of your home kitchen.

Whether you're a passionate foodie, a budding chef, or someone simply looking to embark on a delicious journey, this book is designed to be your guide, offering step-by-step instructions, tips, and flavorful recipes that cater to beginners and enthusiasts alike.

Join us as we uncover the magic behind homemade pizza, explore its rich history, understand the reasons for its worldwide popularity, and embark on an exciting quest to master the craft of pizzamaking, one delicious slice at a time.

Get ready to roll up your sleeves, embrace the aroma of freshly baked dough, and discover the joy of creating your own mouth watering pizzas—simple, easy, and oh so satisfying.

Indulge in the aromatic world of homemade pizza where dough transforms into a canvas and toppings are brushes of flavor. This cookbook serves as your gateway into the delightful realm of crafting pizzas from scratch, inviting you to explore the simplicity and creativity behind this beloved culinary art.

Join us as we unlock the secrets, techniques, and recipes that bring the magic of homemade pizza straight to your kitchen. Whether you're a novice or a seasoned home cook, this guide is tailored to inspire your culinary journey, offering easy to follow steps and diverse recipes to ignite your passion for creating perfect homemade pizzas.

Prepare to embark on a delicious adventure where dough becomes crust, sauce becomes art, and toppings become your signature masterpiece. Welcome to the enticing world of homemade pizza!

Let's begin this delectable adventure into the world of homemade pizza!

Why Pizza Is So Popular

Pizza's popularity stems from its versatility, universal appeal, and comforting flavors. Its widespread love can be attributed to several factors:

1. Versatility: Pizza offers a canvas for endless creativity. Its adaptable nature allows for diverse toppings, sauces, and crust styles, catering to a wide range of tastes and dietary preferences.

2. Ease of Customization: Individuals can personalize their pizzas, tailoring them to their specific cravings or dietary needs, making it a universally loved dish.

3. Social Food: Pizza is inherently a communal food, often shared among friends and family. Its ability to bring people together around a table enhances its appeal as a social and enjoyable meal.

4. Ease of Accessibility: Found in nearly every corner of the world, pizza is easily available, whether from local pizzerias, restaurants, or made at home.

5. Comfort Food: Its combination of gooey cheese, savory toppings, and crispy crust provides a comforting, satisfying experience that transcends cultural boundaries.

6. Culinary Evolution: Despite its origins in Italy, pizza has evolved globally, adopting various regional influences, resulting in an array of unique flavors and styles.

In essence, pizza's popularity rests on its adaptability, communal nature, and ability to cater to diverse tastes, making it a beloved comfort food enjoyed by people worldwide.

Who This Book Is For?

The "Easy Pizza Cookbook" is designed for a broad audience, catering to:

1. Beginners: Individuals new to pizzamaking who want to learn the basics, step-by-step , from dough preparation to assembling and baking their own delicious pizzas at home.

2. Home Cooks: Those seeking inspiration and guidance to elevate their pizzamaking skills with creative recipes, techniques, and tips to experiment with flavors and textures.

3. Food Enthusiasts: People passionate about exploring diverse culinary experiences, wanting to delve deeper into the art of crafting homemade pizzas, discovering new flavors, and expanding their cooking repertoire.

4. Entrepreneurs: Aspiring individuals interested in starting their homemade pizza business, this book provides insights into the craft, along with tips on setting up, marketing, and running a successful pizza venture.

5. Anyone Who Loves Pizza: Ultimately, this book is for anyone who appreciates the deliciousness of pizza, offering a variety of recipes and techniques to create mouthwatering pizzas that satisfy a range of tastes and preferences.

Whether you're a novice eager to learn, a home cook seeking new recipes, or an entrepreneur envisioning a pizza business, this cookbook welcomes you to explore the joys of making and enjoying homemade pizzas.

How This Book Is Organized

The "Easy Pizza Cookbook" is meticulously organized to guide readers through a comprehensive journey in pizzamaking. Here's how this book is structured:

1. Introduction: Welcoming readers to the world of homemade pizza, providing an overview of what to expect and the reasons behind pizza's popularity.

2. Chapter Breakdown: Divided into several chapters, each focusing on crucial aspects of pizzamaking:

- Pizza Basics

An introduction to pizza's history, types, essential ingredients, and tools needed for successful pizza preparation.

- Homemade Pizza Dough

Exploring various dough recipes, including classic, quick, and specialty options, accompanied by tips for perfecting the dough.

- Pizza Sauces

A detailed guide on preparing different sauces such as classic tomato, pesto, white sauce, and others, emphasizing their role in enhancing pizza flavors.

- Pizza Toppings

Exploring traditional and innovative topping options, from meats and vegetables to cheeses, enabling readers to create their ideal pizza combinations.

- Assembling Your Pizza

Step-by-step instructions on rolling out dough, applying sauce, arranging toppings, and achieving a perfect cheese distribution for an impeccable pizza.

- Baking and Cooking Techniques

Guidance on various cooking methods such as oven baking, grilling, and using specialized tools for different pizza styles.

- Special Pizza Recipes

A collection of diverse pizza recipes including classics like Margherita, Pepperoni, and unique variations like seafood and dessert pizzas.

- Tips and Tricks

Insights on perfecting the crust, experimenting with flavors, accommodating dietary restrictions, and storing/reheating pizzas.

- Homemade Pizza Business

Information for those interested in turning their passion for pizza-making into a business, covering licensing, marketing, and customer relations.

- Troubleshooting and FAQs

Common mistakes, quick solutions, and frequently asked questions to aid readers in overcoming challenges during the pizzamaking process.

3. Conclusion: Wrapping up the journey, encouraging readers to continue exploring homemade pizzamaking and inviting them to share their creations.

4. Appendices: Additional resources such as a recipe index, measurement conversion tables, recommended readings, and a glossary for easy reference.

5. Index: A quick reference guide to key topics covered in the book for convenient navigation.

This organized structure allows readers to follow a logical progression, from the fundamentals to more advanced techniques, ensuring a comprehensive understanding of crafting delicious homemade pizzas.

Pizza Basics: Exploring the Heart of Pizza-Making

The Essence of Pizza: A Culinary Classic

Pizza stands as a versatile, globally adored dish known for its delectable flavors and comforting appeal. At its core, it's a savory delight born from simple ingredients, offering a canvas for creativity and culinary innovation.

A Brief History of Pizza: From Humble Beginnings to Global Icon

- **Origins in Naples, Italy**

Pizza's journey began in Naples, Italy, in the late 18th century. Initially, it was a simple and affordable dish favored by the working class. The original Neapolitan pizza featured a basic flatbread topped with tomatoes, mozzarella cheese, and olive oil—a nourishing meal that quickly gained popularity in the streets of Naples.

- **Evolution and Popularity**

As pizza's popularity grew within Naples, it underwent evolution both in ingredients and preparation methods. The addition of basil leaves and various other toppings paved the way for diverse pizza varieties, each reflecting the tastes and preferences of different regions within Italy.

- **Margherita Pizza's Royal Connection**

The iconic Margherita pizza, featuring tomatoes, mozzarella, and basil, holds a special place in pizza history. Legend has it that in 1889, pizzaiolo Raffaele Esposito created this pizza in honor of Queen Margherita of Savoy, incorporating the colors of the Italian flag. Its royal endorsement catapulted the Margherita to fame, solidifying its status as a classic.

- **Global Spread and Adaptation**

In the late 19th and early 20th centuries, Italian immigrants carried their culinary traditions—including pizza—to various parts of the world. Over time, pizza evolved to reflect the tastes of different cultures, resulting in a plethora of regional variations. From the New York Style thin crust to the deep dish pizzas of Chicago, each region put its unique twist on this beloved dish.

- **Cultural Impact and Icon Status**

Pizza's evolution from a humble street food to a globally recognized dish underscores its cultural significance. Its presence in popular culture, movies, and art further solidifies its status as an iconic and universally loved food, transcending borders and connecting people through shared enjoyment.

Continued Evolution

Even today, pizza continues to evolve, with chefs and home cooks experimenting with new ingredients, unique flavor combinations, and alternative crusts to cater to diverse tastes and dietary preferences.

This historical journey of pizza from its modest origins in Naples to its status as a globally adored dish showcases its cultural significance, adaptability, and enduring appeal across centuries and continents.

Types of Pizza: From Classic to Creative

Classic Varieties

- Margherita

Originating from Naples, Italy, this pizza features simple yet vibrant flavors—tomato sauce, fresh mozzarella cheese, basil leaves, and olive oil—representing the colors of the Italian flag.

- Neapolitan

Known for its adherence to tradition, the Neapolitan pizza boasts simplicity with its thin crust, minimal toppings of

San Marzano tomatoes, mozzarella cheese, basil, and olive oil, baked in a woodfired oven.

Regional Variations

- New York-Style Pizza

Characterized by its large, foldable slices with a thin yet slightly chewy crust. Toppings typically include tomato sauce and mozzarella, often with pepperoni or other toppings.

- Chicago Deep-Dish Pizza

A thick, deep dish crust filled with layers of cheese, toppings like sausage or vegetables, and a rich tomato sauce, offering a hearty and filling pizza experience.

Italian Regional Pizzas

- Sicilian Pizza

Featuring a thick, rectangular crust with a hearty layer of tomato sauce, often topped with onions, anchovies, and a dusting of Pecorino cheese.

- Pizza Romana

Characterized by a thin, crispy crust topped with ingredients such as tomatoes, mozzarella, and a variety of vegetables or cured meats.

Creative and Specialty Pizzas

- Seafood Pizza

A delightful combination of seafood ingredients like shrimp, calamari, and mussels atop a traditional pizza base, offering a taste of the ocean's flavors.

- BBQ Chicken Pizza

Highlighting barbecue sauce, chicken, red onions, and a blend of cheeses, this pizza offers a tangy, savory twist to traditional flavors.

Vegetarian and Vegan Options

- Vegetarian Pizza

Featuring an abundance of fresh vegetables, such as bell peppers, onions, mushrooms, olives, and artichokes, catering to those preferring a plant based option.

- Vegan Pizza

Utilizing plant based cheeses, a variety of vegetables, and innovative toppings to create a satisfying and cruelty free pizza experience.

Innovative and Fusion Pizzas

- Breakfast Pizza

Incorporating breakfast ingredients like eggs, bacon, or sausage, turning pizza into a delightful morning treat.

- Global Fusion Pizzas

Infusing flavors from various cuisines, such as Thai Inspired pizzas with peanut sauce, chicken, and vegetables, showcasing creativity in flavor combinations.

Ingredients You'll Need

1. Pizza Dough Ingredients
   - Flour: All Purpose or bread flour for the dough base.
   - Yeast: Active dry or instant yeast for leavening.
   - Salt: Essential for flavor enhancement.
   - Water/Olive Oil: For dough hydration and texture.

2. Pizza Sauce Ingredients
   - Canned Tomatoes: San Marzano or plum tomatoes for sauce base.
   - Garlic/Onion: Flavor enhancers for the sauce.
   - Herbs and Spices: Basil, oregano, salt, pepper for seasoning.

3. Pizza Toppings
   - Mozzarella Cheese: Fresh or shredded for classic pizza texture.
   - Vegetables: Tomatoes, bell peppers, onions, mushrooms, olives, etc.

- Meats: Pepperoni, sausage, ham, bacon, chicken, etc.
- Herbs and Greens: Fresh basil, arugula, spinach, etc., for added freshness.

4. Additional Flavor Enhancers
   - Olive Oil: Drizzling over the pizza for added richness.
   - Parmesan Cheese: Grated for extra flavor.
   - Chili Flakes/Garlic Powder: Optional for added spice or flavor depth.

Essential Kitchen Tools

1. Mixing and Preparing Dough
   - Mixing Bowls: For combining and kneading dough ingredients.
   - Measuring Cups/Spoons: Accurately measure flour, water, yeast, etc.
   - Dough Scraper: Helps in handling and shaping dough.

2. Pizza Preparation and Baking
   - Pizza Stone or Baking Sheet: For even baking and crispy crust.
   - Pizza Peel: To slide pizza in and out of the oven/grill.

- Rolling Pin: For rolling out dough to desired thickness.
- Pizza Cutter: Easily slices through the finished pizza.

3. Cooking and Baking Equipment

- Oven or Grill: For baking pizzas at high temperatures.
- Cast Iron Skillet: Alternative for pan pizzas or unique crusts.
- Pizza Cutter or Wheel: Ensures clean and easy slicing of cooked pizzas.

4. Miscellaneous

- Kitchen Towels: For cleaning and covering dough while resting.
- Parchment Paper/Cornmeal: Prevents dough sticking to surfaces while baking.
- Timer/Thermometer: Ensures accurate cooking times and temperatures.

These essential ingredients and kitchen tools are fundamental for preparing homemade pizzas, allowing for the creation of flavorful dough, delicious sauces, diverse toppings, and the necessary equipment to achieve professional quality homemade pizzas.

Preparing Your Work-station for Pizza-Making Success

1. Clear and Clean Surfaces
   - Clean Countertops: Ensure your work area is clean and sanitized before starting.
   - Ample Space: Clear sufficient space for rolling out dough and assembling pizzas.

2. Gather Ingredients and Tools
   - Organize Ingredients: Arrange all required ingredients within reach for easy access while preparing the pizza.
   - Prepare Toppings: Wash, chop, and prepare toppings in advance to streamline the assembly process.
   - Measure Ingredients: Pre-measure ingredients to avoid last minute hassles.

3. Preheat Oven and Equipment
   - Preheat Oven: Set the oven or grill to the recommended temperature for baking pizzas.

- Prepare Pizza Stone or Baking Sheet: Place the pizza stone or baking sheet in the oven while preheating for even heat distribution.

4. Dough Preparation Area
- Flour Surface: Lightly flour your work surface to prevent dough from sticking while rolling it out.
- Rolling Pin: Have a rolling pin ready to roll out the dough to your desired thickness.

5. Assembling Station
- Parchment Paper/Cornmeal: Use parchment paper or cornmeal on a pizza peel to easily transfer assembled pizzas to the oven.
- Sauce and Toppings: Have bowls for pizza sauce and separate containers for various toppings to easily access and assemble pizzas.

6. Kitchen Tools and Utensils
- Pizza Peel or Sheet Pan: Prepare the pizza peel or sheet pan with parchment paper for assembling and transferring pizzas.
- Pizza Cutter or Wheel: Keep a pizza cutter or wheel nearby for slicing the finished pizza.

7. Timers and Accessories

- Kitchen Timer: Set a timer to keep track of baking time for a perfectly cooked pizza.
- Oven Mitts: Have oven mitts or kitchen towels ready to handle hot pans and baking sheets.

8. Cleaning Supplies

- Clean Cloth/Towels: Keep damp towels or cloths nearby for quick cleanup during and after the pizza-making process.
- Sink Access: Ensure easy access to a sink for washing hands and utensils as needed.

9. Create an Enjoyable Atmosphere

- Music or Ambiance: Play some music or set a pleasant ambiance to make the pizzamaking process more enjoyable and fun.

Preparing your workstation ahead of time ensures a smooth and enjoyable pizzamaking experience, allowing for efficient assembly, baking, and cleanup, leading to delicious homemade pizzas with ease.

Step One

Crafting Homemade Pizza Dough

Rolling Out the Dough

1. Prepare Your Work Surface
   - Sprinkle some flour on a clean, dry surface.
   - This will prevent the dough from sticking as you roll it out.

2. Shape the Dough
   - Place your prepared pizza dough on the floured surface.
   - Using your hands, gently flatten it into a disk shape.

3. Start Rolling
   - Use a rolling pin to start rolling the dough outwards from the center.
   - Roll in one direction and then rotate the dough a quarter turn.
   - Repeat this process until you achieve your desired thickness.

4. Maintain Even Thickness

- Aim for an even thickness across the entire surface of the dough.
- Ensure it's thin enough to your liking but not too thin that it becomes difficult to handle.

5. Transfer to Pizza Pan or Stone

- Once rolled out, transfer the dough to a pizza pan, stone, or parchment paper for assembly.
- Ensure it fits the pan or stone without stretching.

Ingredients

- Flour: 2½- 3 cups of all-purpose or bread flour.
- Yeast: 1 packet (2¼ teaspoons) of active dry yeast or instant yeast.
- Sugar: 1 teaspoon of granulated sugar.
- Salt: 1 teaspoon for flavor enhancement.
- Water: 1 cup of warm water (approximately 110°F/43°C).
- Olive Oil: 2 tablespoons for dough texture and flavor.

Instructions

1. Activate the Yeast
   - In a small bowl, combine the warm water, sugar, and yeast.
   - Stir gently and let it sit for about 5-10 minutes until it becomes frothy or foamy.

2. Prepare the Dough Mixture
   - In a large mixing bowl, combine the flour and salt.
   - Create a well in the center of the flour mixture and pour in the activated yeast mixture and olive oil.

3. Knead the Dough
   - Using a wooden spoon or your hands, mix the ingredients until a shaggy dough forms.
   - Transfer the dough to a lightly floured surface and knead for about 57 minutes until it becomes smooth, elastic, and no longer sticky.
   - Add more flour if needed to prevent sticking.

4. First Rise
   - Place the dough in a lightly oiled bowl, cover it with a damp cloth or plastic wrap, and let it rise in a warm, draft free place for about 11.5 hours, or until it doubles in size.

5. Punch Down and Shape

- Once the dough has risen, gently punch it down to release air bubbles.
- Divide the dough into portions (as needed for your desired pizza size) and shape each portion into a ball. Use immediately or store for later use.

6. Final Notes

- If using the dough immediately, allow it to rest for about 10-15 minutes before rolling it out.
- If storing, wrap each dough ball tightly in plastic wrap and refrigerate for up to 12 days.
- Alternatively, freeze for longer storage, thawing it in the refrigerator before use.

Crafting homemade pizza dough lays the foundation for a delicious pizza. Follow these steps to create a versatile and flavorful dough that serves as the base for your homemade pizzas. Adjust the ingredients and techniques based on your preferred pizza style and desired crust thickness.

Pizza dough recipe

1. Classic Pizza Dough Recipe

Ingredients

- All-purpose Flour: 3 ½ cups
- Warm Water: 1⅓ cups (approximately 110°F/43°C)
- Active Dry Yeast: 2 ¼ teaspoons (1 packet)
- Granulated Sugar: 1 teaspoon
- Salt: 1 ½ teaspoons
- Olive Oil: 2 tablespoons

Instructions

1. Activate the Yeast

- In a small bowl, combine warm water, sugar, and yeast.
- Stir gently and let it sit for about 5-10 minutes until the mixture becomes frothy or foamy.

2. Mix the Dough

- In a large mixing bowl, combine the flour and salt. Make a well in the center of the flour mixture.
- Pour the activated yeast mixture and olive oil into the well.

3. Kneading Process

- Stir the ingredients together until a shaggy dough forms.
- Transfer the dough to a lightly floured surface and knead for about 8-10 minutes until it becomes smooth, elastic, and slightly tacky.
- Add more flour if needed to prevent sticking.

4. First Rise

- Place the dough in a lightly oiled bowl, turning to coat all sides with oil. Cover the bowl with plastic wrap or a damp cloth.
- Allow the dough to rise in a warm, draft free place for about 11.5 hours, or until it doubles in size.

5. Prepare for Pizza Making

- Once risen, gently punch down the dough to release air bubbles.
- Divide the dough into portions (depending on your desired pizza size) and shape each portion into a ball.

6. Resting Period

- Place the dough balls on a floured surface, cover them with a kitchen towel, and let them rest for an additional 15-20 minutes before rolling them out or stretching them into pizza crusts.

7. Rolling or Stretching
- Use a rolling pin or your hands to shape and stretch the dough into the desired thickness and size for your pizzas.

8. Pizza Assembly
- Add your favorite sauce, toppings, and cheese onto the prepared pizza dough before baking according to your pizza recipe.

9. Baking Instructions
- Preheat your oven to the highest temperature (usually around 500°F/260°C) and bake the pizza on a pizza stone or baking sheet for 10-15 minutes or until the crust is golden brown and the cheese is melted and bubbly.

10. Serve and Enjoy
- Once baked, remove the pizza from the oven, slice it, and savor the delicious flavors of your homemade classic pizza.

This classic pizza dough recipe provides a versatile and delicious base for creating homemade pizzas. Adjust the thickness and size of the crust according to your preferences and enjoy experimenting with various toppings and flavors.

2. Quick and Easy Pizza Dough Recipe

Ingredients

- All-purpose Flour: 2 ½ cups
- Baking Powder: 1 tablespoon
- Salt: ½ teaspoon
- Olive Oil: 2 tablespoons
- Warm Water: 1 cup (approximately 110°F/43°C)

Instructions

1. Prepare the Dough

- In a mixing bowl, combine the all-purpose flour, baking powder, and salt.
- Mix well to ensure even distribution of ingredients.

2. Add Wet Ingredients

- Create a well in the center of the dry ingredients and pour in the olive oil and warm water.

3. Mix and Knead

- Stir the ingredients together until a shaggy dough forms.
- Transfer the dough onto a lightly floured surface and knead for about 35 minutes until the dough is smooth and elastic.

4. Rest the Dough

- Cover the dough with a clean kitchen towel or plastic wrap and let it rest for 10-15 minutes.
- This resting period helps relax the gluten and makes the dough easier to handle.

5. Roll Out the Dough

- After resting, roll out the dough using a rolling pin to your desired thickness and shape for your pizza.

6. Pizza Assembly and Baking

- Add your favorite sauce, cheese, and toppings onto the prepared pizza dough.
- Pre-heat your oven to the highest temperature (around 500°F/260°C).
- Transfer the assembled pizza onto a baking sheet or pizza stone and bake for 10-15 minutes, or until the

crust is golden brown and the toppings are cooked to your liking.

7. Serve and Enjoy
- Once baked, remove the pizza from the oven, slice it, and relish your quick and easy homemade pizza!

This quick and straightforward pizza dough recipe allows you to whip up delicious homemade pizzas in no time. Experiment with different toppings and enjoy a freshly baked pizza straight from your oven! Adjust the thickness and baking time based on your desired crust texture.

3. Gluten-Free Pizza Dough Recipe

Ingredients
- GlutenFree Flour Blend: 2 ½ cups (a mix of rice flour, tapioca flour, and potato starch)
- Xanthan Gum: 2 teaspoons (if not included in the flour blend)
- Instant Yeast: 2 ¼ teaspoons (1 packet)
- Sugar: 1 teaspoon
- Salt: 1 teaspoon
- Olive Oil: 2 tablespoons
- Warm Water: 1 cup (approximately 110°F/43°C)

Instructions

1. Activate the Yeast

- In a small bowl, combine warm water, sugar, and yeast.
- Allow it to sit for 5-10 minutes until it becomes frothy.

2. Mix the Dough

- In a mixing bowl, combine the gluten free flour blend, xanthan gum (if not in the flour mix), and salt.
- Create a well in the center and pour in the activated yeast mixture and olive oil.

3. Knead the Dough

- Mix the ingredients until a dough forms.
- Knead the dough on a surface dusted with gluten-free flour for about 57 minutes until smooth and elastic.

4. First Rise

- Place the dough in a lightly oiled bowl, cover it with plastic wrap or a damp cloth, and let it rise in a warm place for 11.5 hours, or until it doubles in size.

5. Prepare for Pizza Making

- Once risen, punch down the dough and divide it into portions for your pizzas.
- Roll out or shape each portion into a pizza crust.

6. Assemble and Bake

- Add sauce, cheese, and toppings to the prepared gluten free pizza crust.
- Bake in a preheated oven at 450°F/230°C for about 12-15 minutes or until the crust is golden and toppings are cooked.

4. Whole Wheat Pizza Dough Recipe

Ingredients
- Whole Wheat Flour: 3 cups
- Instant Yeast: 2 ¼ teaspoons (1 packet)
- Honey or Maple Syrup: 1 tablespoon
- Salt: 1 teaspoon
- Olive Oil: 2 tablespoons
- Warm Water: 1 ¼ cups (approximately 110°F/43°C)

Instructions
1. Activate the Yeast
- In a bowl, combine warm water, honey or maple syrup, and yeast.

- Let it sit for 5-10 minutes until frothy.

2. Mix and Knead

- In a mixing bowl, combine the whole wheat flour and salt.
- Make a well in the center and pour in the activated yeast mixture and olive oil.
- Mix until a dough forms, then knead the dough on a floured surface for about 57 minutes until it becomes smooth and elastic.

3. First Rise

- Place the dough in a lightly oiled bowl, cover it, and let it rise in a warm place for 11.5 hours, or until it doubles in size.

4. Prepare and Bake

- Once risen, punch down the dough and divide it into portions for your pizzas.
- Roll out or shape each portion into a pizza crust.
- Add sauce, cheese, and toppings, then bake in a preheated oven at 450°F/230°C for about 12-15 minutes or until the crust is golden and toppings are cooked.

These recipes offer alternatives for gluten free and whole wheat pizza dough, providing options for those with dietary preferences or restrictions. Adjust the toppings and baking times according to personal preferences for a delightful homemade pizza experience.

Tips for Perfect Pizza Dough

1. Use High-Quality Ingredients
   - Opt for high quality flour, fresh yeast, and good olive oil.
   - Quality ingredients contribute to better flavor and texture.

2. Proper Yeast Activation
   - Activate yeast in warm water (110°F/43°C) with a bit of sugar. This step ensures the yeast is alive and ready to leaven the dough.

3. Kneading Technique
   - Knead the dough properly to develop gluten. This process helps create a good structure and texture in the dough.
   - Knead until the dough becomes smooth and elastic.

4. Rising Time and Temperature

- Allow the dough to rise in a warm, draft free environment.
- Proper rising time (usually 11.5 hours) allows the dough to double in size, ensuring a light and airy crust.

5. Resting Periods

- Let the dough rest after kneading and before shaping.
- This allows the gluten to relax, making the dough easier to handle.

6. Correct Dough Consistency

- Aim for a slightly sticky and soft dough. It should be tacky but not overly wet.
- Adjust flour or water as needed to achieve the right consistency.

7. Proper Dough Portioning

- Divide the dough into equal portions for consistent sized pizzas.
- This ensures even baking and a balanced ratio of toppings to crust.

8. Rolling or Stretching Technique
- Gently roll or stretch the dough to the desired thickness, ensuring an even surface.
- Avoid excessive handling or pressing that can deflate the dough.

9. Poke Air Bubbles
- Before adding toppings, gently poke air bubbles on the surface of the rolledout dough to prevent large bubbles from forming during baking.

10. Preheat Oven and Baking Surface
- Preheat your oven and pizza stone or baking sheet thoroughly.
- A hot oven and surface contribute to a crisp bottom crust.

11. Use Cornmeal or Parchment Paper
- Sprinkle cornmeal on the pizza peel or use parchment paper to prevent the dough from sticking during transfer to the oven.

12. Avoid Overloading Toppings

- Don't overload the pizza with toppings, as this can weigh down the dough and make it soggy. Balance the amount of toppings for a well cooked crust.

13. Monitor Baking Time

- Keep an eye on the pizza while it bakes.
- Oven temperatures can vary, so adjust baking time accordingly to achieve the desired level of crispness and browning.

14. Rest Before Slicing

- Allow the freshly baked pizza to rest for a few minutes before slicing.
- This helps the toppings set and prevents them from sliding off.

15. Practice and Experiment

- Practice makes perfect!
- Experiment with different recipes, techniques, and baking times to find what works best for your preferences.

By following these tips, you can improve the quality and consistency of your pizza dough, leading to delicious homemade pizzas that rival those from your favorite pizzeria. Adjust and fine-tune these tips based on your personal preferences and oven capabilities.

Step Two

Pizza Sauces

Spreading the Sauce

1. Select Your Sauce
   - Choose your preferred pizza sauce, whether it's tomato based, white sauce, pesto, or any other sauce you prefer.

2. Sauce Application
   - Using a ladle or spoon, scoop an appropriate amount of sauce onto the center of the rolled out dough.

3. Spread Evenly
   - With the back of the ladle or a spoon, start spreading the sauce in a circular motion from the center outward, leaving a small border around the edges for the crust.

4. Even Distribution
   - Ensure the sauce is spread evenly to avoid creating areas with too much or too little sauce.

44

5. Moderation is Key

- Don't oversauce the pizza, as an excess of sauce can make the dough soggy.
- Start with a moderate amount and add more if needed.

6. Consider Flavor Balance

- If using multiple sauces or layering different flavors, be mindful of balancing the flavors to complement the toppings.

1. Classic Tomato Pizza Sauce

Ingredients

- Canned Crushed Tomatoes: 1 can (28 ounces)
- Olive Oil: 2 tablespoons
- Garlic: 2 cloves, minced
- Dried Basil: 1 teaspoon
- Dried Oregano: 1 teaspoon
- Salt and Pepper: To taste
- Sugar: 1 teaspoon (optional, to balance acidity)

Instructions

1. Heat olive oil in a saucepan over medium heat.
2. Add minced garlic and sauté for a minute until fragrant.

3. Pour in crushed tomatoes, dried basil, dried oregano, salt, pepper, and sugar (if using).

4. Simmer the sauce on low heat for about 15-20 minutes, stirring occasionally, until it thickens to your desired consistency.

5. Let the sauce cool before using it as a pizza base.

2. Pesto Sauce

Ingredients

- Fresh Basil Leaves: 2 cups, packed
- Pine Nuts or Walnuts: ⅓ cup
- Garlic: 2 cloves
- Parmesan Cheese: ½ cup, grated
- Olive Oil: ⅓ cup
- Salt and Pepper: To taste

Instructions

1. In a food processor, blend basil leaves, pine nuts or walnuts, garlic, and parmesan cheese until coarsely chopped.

2. While the processor is running, slowly drizzle in the olive oil until the mixture becomes a smooth paste.

3. Add salt and pepper to taste.

4. Use the pesto sauce as a flavorful alternative to traditional tomato sauce on your pizza.

3. White Pizza Sauce

Ingredients

- Unsalted Butter: 2 tablespoons
- Garlic: 2 cloves, minced
- All-purpose Flour: 2 tablespoons
- Milk: 1 cup
- Parmesan Cheese: ½ cup, grated
- Salt and Pepper: To taste
- Dried Thyme or Oregano: 1 teaspoon (optional)

Instructions

1. Melt butter in a saucepan over medium heat.

2. Add minced garlic and sauté until fragrant.

3. Stir in flour and cook for a minute to form a roux.

4. Gradually whisk in the milk, stirring constantly until the mixture thickens.

5. Add grated parmesan cheese, salt, pepper, and dried herbs (if using). Stir until the cheese melts and the sauce is smooth.

6. Let the white sauce cool before spreading it on your pizza dough.

4. Barbecue Sauce

Ingredients
- Ketchup: 1 cup
- Apple Cider Vinegar: 2 tablespoons
- Brown Sugar: 2 tablespoons
- Worcestershire Sauce: 1 tablespoon
- Garlic Powder: 1 teaspoon
- Paprika: 1 teaspoon
- Onion Powder: 1 teaspoon
- Salt and Pepper: To taste

Instructions
1. In a saucepan, combine ketchup, apple cider vinegar, brown sugar, Worcestershire sauce, garlic powder, paprika, onion powder, salt, and pepper.

2. Simmer the mixture over low heat for 1015 minutes, stirring occasionally, until it thickens and flavors meld together.

3. Allow the barbecue sauce to cool before using it as a pizza sauce.

5. White Pizza Sauce

Ingredients

- Unsalted Butter: 3 tablespoons
- All-purpose Flour: 3 tablespoons
- Garlic: 2 cloves, minced
- Milk: 1 ½ cups
- Salt: ½ teaspoon
- Black Pepper: ¼ teaspoon
- Dried Thyme or Oregano: ½ teaspoon (optional)
- Grated Parmesan Cheese: ½ cup

Instructions

1. Melt butter in a saucepan over medium heat.

2. Add minced garlic and sauté until fragrant, about 1 minute.

3. Sprinkle flour into the saucepan, stirring constantly for about 12 minutes to make a roux.

4. Gradually pour in the milk while whisking continuously to avoid lumps.

5. Cook the mixture until it thickens, around 34 minutes, stirring frequently.

6. Add salt, black pepper, dried thyme or oregano (if using), and grated parmesan cheese. Stir until the cheese is melted and the sauce is smooth.

7. Remove from heat and let the sauce cool before using it as a pizza base.

6. BBQ Sauce

Ingredients
- Ketchup: 1 cup
- Apple Cider Vinegar: ¼ cup
- Brown Sugar: ¼ cup, packed
- Worcestershire Sauce: 2 tablespoons
- Dijon Mustard: 1 tablespoon
- Paprika: 1 teaspoon
- Garlic Powder: ½ teaspoon
- Onion Powder: ½ teaspoon
- Liquid Smoke: ½ teaspoon (optional)
- Cayenne Pepper or Hot Sauce: ¼ teaspoon (adjust to taste)
- Salt: ½ teaspoon
- Black Pepper: ¼ teaspoon

Instructions

1. In a saucepan, combine ketchup, apple cider vinegar, brown sugar, Worcestershire sauce, Dijon mustard, paprika, garlic powder, onion powder, liquid smoke (if using), cayenne pepper or hot sauce, salt, and black pepper.

2. Bring the mixture to a gentle simmer over medium heat, stirring occasionally to dissolve the sugar.

3. Reduce the heat to low and let the sauce cook for 1015 minutes, allowing the flavors to meld together.

4. Taste and adjust seasoning if necessary.

5. Let the BBQ sauce cool before using it as a pizza sauce or for dipping.

7. Unique Sauce Ideas

1. Alfredo Sauce
- Create a creamy Alfredo sauce by combining heavy cream, butter, garlic, grated parmesan cheese, salt, and pepper.
- Simmer until thickened and use it as a white pizza sauce alternative.

2. Buffalo Sauce
- Mix hot sauce (like Frank's RedHot), melted butter, a splash of vinegar, and garlic powder for a spicy and tangy Buffalo sauce.
- Ideal for chicken-based or vegetarian pizzas.

3. Pesto Mayo Sauce

- Blend basil pesto with mayonnaise for a creamy and herbaceous sauce.
- It works well as a drizzle or dollop on finished pizzas.

4. Chipotle Tomato Sauce
- Combine crushed tomatoes with chipotle peppers in adobo sauce, garlic, cumin, and a touch of honey for a smoky and slightly spicy pizza sauce.

5. Hummus Spread
- Use hummus as a base for a Mediterranean Inspired pizza.
- Spread it on the dough and top with roasted vegetables, feta cheese, olives, and fresh herbs.

Perfecting the Sauce

1. Simmer for Flavor
- Allow your sauce to simmer gently to meld the flavors.
- Simmering also helps reduce excess moisture, preventing a soggy pizza crust.

2. Seasoning Balance

- Taste your sauce as it cooks and adjust seasoning accordingly.
- Add a pinch of sugar to balance acidity or more herbs/spices for depth of flavor.

3. Consistency Control

- If your sauce is too thin, continue simmering to reduce it to the desired thickness.
- Conversely, if it's too thick, adjust by adding a bit of water or broth.

4. Cool Down Before Use

- Let the sauce cool completely before spreading it on the pizza dough.
- Hot sauce can cause the dough to become soggy.

5. Layering Flavors

- Layer the sauce thinly on the dough, leaving space at the edges for the crust to crisp.
- Avoid overloading the sauce, as excess moisture can make the pizza soggy.

6. Preparation in Advance

- Prepare the sauce ahead of time and allow it to cool completely.

- Store it in an airtight container in the refrigerator for up to a few days, letting the flavors further develop.

7. Experiment and Personalize
- Don't be afraid to experiment with different ingredients and combinations to create your signature sauce.
- Adjust quantities and ingredients to suit your taste preferences.

By exploring unique sauce ideas and focusing on the perfect balance of flavors and consistency, you can enhance the taste profile of your homemade pizzas, offering a variety of exciting flavors to delight your taste buds!

Step Three

Pizza Toppings

Layering toppings and distributing cheese evenly play crucial roles in crafting a delicious pizza. Here's a guide to masterfully layering toppings and achieving ideal cheese distribution:

1. Meat and Hearty Ingredients First
   - Start with heavier toppings like meats (pepperoni, sausage, etc.) or ingredients that need more time to cook.
   - Distribute them evenly across the sauced pizza dough.

2. Vegetables and Lighter Toppings Next
   - Layer your vegetables (bell peppers, onions, mushrooms) and lighter toppings over the meat.
   - Spread them out to ensure even coverage.

3. Leafy Greens and Herbs After Baking
   - Fresh herbs (like basil) or leafy greens (spinach, arugula) should generally be added after the pizza is baked to avoid wilting or burning.

- Sprinkle them as a finishing touch.

4. Even Distribution
- Aim for an equal distribution of toppings across the entire pizza to ensure every slice offers a balanced flavor profile.

The Art of Cheese Distribution

1. Selecting the Right Cheese
- Choose the type of cheese or cheese blend that complements your toppings. Mozzarella is a classic choice, but mixing cheeses can enhance flavors.

2. Even Cheese Coverage
- Sprinkle the cheese evenly over the layered toppings.
- Start from the center and work your way towards the edges to ensure consistent coverage.

3. Moderation and Balance
- Avoid overloading the pizza with cheese.
- A moderate amount ensures it melts evenly and doesn't overpower the other flavors.

4. Cheese Blending

- If using multiple cheeses, mix them together before sprinkling to create a harmonious flavor profile.

5. Edge Leave for the Crust
- Leave a small border (about 1/2 to 1 inch) around the edges of the pizza without cheese to allow the crust to bake golden and crispy.

6. Experiment with Cheese Placement
- Consider layering some cheese underneath the toppings and some on top.
- This can help "glue" the toppings to the pizza and prevent them from sliding off.

Additional Tips
- Consider grating fresh cheese for better meltability and flavor.
- Don't be afraid to experiment with different cheese quantities and combinations to find your preferred taste.

By layering your toppings strategically and ensuring even cheese distribution, you can create a visually appealing and flavor packed pizza. Balancing flavors and textures is key to achieving a perfect homemade pizza! Adjust the toppings and cheese quantities to suit your taste preferences.

Whether you're a fan of classic combinations or looking to explore gourmet or vegetarian options, there's a wide array of toppings to suit every taste bud. Mix and match these toppings based on your preferences to create a personalized pizza masterpiece!

Here's a diverse list of pizza toppings that you can mix and match to create your perfect pizza:

- **Classic Pizza Toppings**

1. Pepperoni: Thinly sliced cured pork sausage.
2. Mozzarella Cheese: Fresh or shredded for that classic pizza cheese.
3. Mushrooms: Sliced button or cremini mushrooms for an earthy flavor.
4. Bell Peppers: Red, green, or yellow peppers, thinly sliced.
5. Onions: Red, white, or caramelized onions add savory sweetness.
6. Italian Sausage: Cooked and crumbled sausage, spicy or mild.
7. Black Olives: Pitted and sliced for a briny taste.

8. Fresh Basil: Adds a refreshing herbaceous note when placed on the pizza after baking.

9. Tomatoes: Sliced tomatoes or cherry tomatoes for freshness.

10. Garlic: Thinly sliced or minced for an aromatic touch.

- **Gourmet and Unique Toppings**

1. Prosciutto: Thinly sliced cured ham adds a savory element.

2. Arugula: Fresh, peppery greens to sprinkle on top after baking.

3. Artichoke Hearts: Canned or marinated, chopped for a tangy addition.

4. Pineapple: For a controversial yet delightful sweet and savory combination.

5. Feta Cheese: Adds a tangy and salty flavor profile.

6. SunDried Tomatoes: Intensely flavored tomatoes for a burst of tanginess.

7. Brie Cheese: Creamy and rich, cut into small pieces for added luxury.

8. Anchovies: For those who enjoy the intense umami flavor.

9. Caramelized Apples: Thinly sliced and caramelized for a sweet twist.

10. Goat Cheese: Tangy and creamy, perfect for adding variety to cheese blends.

- **Vegetarian and Vegan Options**

1. Spinach: Fresh or sautéed for a leafy green addition.
2. Broccoli: Blanched or roasted broccoli florets for texture.
3. Zucchini: Sliced thinly for a mild and fresh topping.
4. Vegan Cheese: Options made from nuts, soy, or tapioca for dairy free alternatives.
5. Tofu or Tempeh: Marinated and crumbled for plant based protein.
6. Roasted Red Peppers: Adds a smoky sweetness to the pizza.
7. Pesto: A flavorful alternative to tomato based sauces.
8. Kalamata Olives: Provides a briny and intense flavor.

- **Traditional Pizza Toppings**

1. Pepperoni: Thinly sliced, spicy cured pork sausage.
2. Italian Sausage: Cooked and crumbled, often seasoned with herbs and spices.
3. Mushrooms: Sliced button or cremini mushrooms for an earthy taste.
4. Green Bell Peppers: Fresh and crunchy, sliced into strips.

5. Onions: Red, white, or caramelized onions for sweetness and depth of flavor.

6. Black Olives: Sliced and pitted, offering a briny taste.

7. Mozzarella Cheese: Shredded or fresh, the classic pizza cheese.

- **Vegetables and Greens for Pizza**

1. Tomatoes: Sliced or diced fresh tomatoes for a burst of flavor.

2. Spinach: Fresh or sautéed spinach leaves for a nutritious addition.

3. Bell Peppers (Various Colors): Red, green, yellow, or orange bell peppers, thinly sliced.

4. Red Onions: Mild and slightly sweet, sliced thinly for a vibrant color.

5. Broccoli: Blanched or roasted broccoli florets for added texture.

6. Zucchini: Sliced into thin rounds or strips for a mild taste.

7. Artichoke Hearts: Canned or marinated artichokes, chopped for a tangy twist.

8. Cherry Tomatoes: Whole or halved cherry tomatoes for a burst of sweetness.

9. Arugula: Fresh, peppery greens to sprinkle on top after baking for freshness.

10. Roasted Garlic: Soft and sweet roasted garlic cloves for depth of flavor.

• Additional Greens and Herbs for Flavor

1. Basil: Fresh basil leaves, torn or chopped, for a classic Italian flavor.

2. Oregano: Dried or fresh oregano leaves for an earthy taste.

3. Rosemary: Fresh rosemary leaves, finely chopped or whole, for a fragrant aroma.

4. Parsley: Chopped fresh parsley to add brightness and freshness.

5. Kale: Finely chopped kale, massaged with olive oil, for a nutrient rich option.

• Meats for Pizza Toppings

1. Pepperoni: Spicy cured pork sausage, thinly sliced.

2. Italian Sausage: Seasoned pork sausage, often crumbled and cooked.

3. Ham: Cooked and sliced ham, offering a savory taste.

4. Bacon: Crispy bacon strips, chopped or crumbled for a smoky flavor.

5. Ground Beef: Cooked and seasoned ground beef for a hearty topping.

6. Chicken: Grilled or roasted chicken breast, sliced or diced.

7. Salami: Dry Cured sausage, thinly sliced for a robust flavor.

8. Prosciutto: Thinly sliced dry cured ham, providing a salty taste.

- **Seafood Options for Pizza**

1. Anchovies: Small, salty fish, usually used sparingly due to their intense flavor.

2. Shrimp: Cooked and deveined shrimp, either whole or chopped.

3. Tuna: Canned or fresh tuna, flaked and spread as a topping.

4. Clams: Minced or whole clams, adding a mild brininess.

5. Calamari: Sliced or diced squid rings, providing a chewy texture.

- **Cheese Varieties for Pizza**

1. Mozzarella: Fresh or shredded, a classic pizza cheese with a mild taste and excellent melting properties.

2. Parmesan: Hard and aged, grated or shaved for a nutty and salty flavor.

3. Cheddar: Sharp and tangy, grated or sliced for added richness.

4. Gouda: Creamy and slightly sweet, grated or thinly sliced for a unique flavor.

5. Fontina: Semi Soft and creamy, offering a buttery and nutty taste.

6. Ricotta: Soft and creamy, dolloped or spread for a mild and slightly sweet addition.

7. Goat Cheese: Tangy and creamy, crumbled or sliced for a distinctive flavor.

8. Blue Cheese: Strong and pungent, crumbled or thinly sliced for a bold taste.

Step Four

Assembling Your Pizza

Assembling a pizza involves a few steps to ensure a delicious outcome. Here's a guide to assembling your pizza:

1. Prepare the Pizza Dough
If using homemade dough, roll it out into the desired shape and thickness on a floured surface. Ensure it fits your pizza pan or stone.

2. Preheat the Oven
Preheat your oven to the highest temperature (usually around 500°F/260°C) for at least 30 minutes. Ensure your pizza stone, if using one, is preheated as well.

3. Prepare the Workstation
Gather all your toppings, sauce, cheese, and any additional ingredients you'll be using.

4. Spread the Sauce
Spread your chosen sauce evenly over the prepared pizza dough, leaving a small border around the edges for the crust.

5. Add Cheese

Sprinkle a generous amount of your preferred cheese(s) over the sauce. Mozzarella is a classic choice, but feel free to mix in other cheeses for additional flavor.

6. Layer the Toppings

Place your chosen meats, vegetables, seafood, and other toppings evenly over the cheese layer. Distribute them according to your taste preferences.

7. Finish with Seasonings and Herbs

Add a final touch of seasonings, such as dried oregano, basil, or red pepper flakes, to enhance the flavors.

8. Transfer to Baking Surface

If using a pizza peel, sprinkle it with cornmeal or use parchment paper to slide the assembled pizza onto the preheated pizza stone or baking sheet.

9. Bake Your Pizza

Carefully transfer the pizza into the preheated oven. Bake for 10-15 minutes or until the crust is golden brown, the cheese is melted, and the toppings are cooked to your liking.

10. Check and Serve

Keep an eye on the pizza as it bakes to prevent burning. Once done, remove it from the oven, let it cool for a few minutes, slice, and serve hot.

Tips

- Even Distribution

Distribute the toppings evenly to ensure a balanced flavor profile.

- Don't Overload

Avoid adding too many toppings as it can make the pizza soggy and difficult to bake properly.

- Experiment

Feel free to mix and match different combinations of toppings to create your favorite flavor profile.

Enjoy the process of assembling your pizza and don't hesitate to get creative with toppings and flavors to tailor the pizza to your taste preferences!

Baking and Cooking Techniques

The baking and cooking techniques significantly impact the final outcome of your pizza. Here's a guide to baking a perfect homemade pizza:

Baking Techniques

1. Preheat Your Oven
   - Preheat your oven to the highest temperature possible, typically around 500°F (260°C) for at least 30 minutes.
   - This ensures a hot oven for proper baking.

2. Use a Pizza Stone or Baking Sheet
   - Place your pizza stone or baking sheet in the preheated oven to warm it up.
   - The hot surface helps create a crispy crust.

3. Properly Transfer the Pizza
   - If using a pizza stone, carefully transfer the assembled pizza onto the hot stone using a pizza peel dusted with cornmeal or parchment paper for easy transfer.

4. Monitor the Baking Time
- Bake the pizza for approximately 10-15 minutes or until the crust is golden brown, the cheese is melted, and the toppings are cooked to your liking.

5. Rotate the Pizza
- Halfway through baking, rotate the pizza 180 degrees to ensure even cooking.
- This helps prevent uneven browning.

6. Keep an Eye on the Oven
- Watch the pizza closely as it bakes to prevent burning.
- Oven temperatures may vary, so adjust baking time accordingly.

Cooking Techniques

1. Cooking the Crust First
- If using a thicker crust or dough, consider partially pre-baking the crust before adding toppings.
- This prevents a soggy crust.

2. Sauté or Precook Certain Ingredients

- Some ingredients, like vegetables or meats with high moisture content, can release excess liquid during baking.
- Pre-cook or sauté these ingredients to remove moisture and enhance flavors.

3. Experiment with Cooking Methods
- Aside from traditional oven baking, try alternative methods like grilling or using a pizza oven if available for a different flavor and texture profile.

4. Personalize Cooking Times
- Adjust the cooking time based on your preference for crust crispness and cheese melt.
- Some prefer a softer crust, while others prefer a crisper finish.

5. Rest Before Slicing
- Let the freshly baked pizza rest for a few minutes before slicing.
- This allows the cheese and toppings to set, making it easier to cut without everything sliding off.

Additional Tips

- For thin crust pizzas, a hotter oven and shorter baking time work best to achieve a crispy crust.
- Keep an oven light on to monitor the pizza without opening the oven door too frequently, which can lower the oven temperature.

By following these baking and cooking techniques, you'll be able to master the art of making a perfectly baked homemade pizza. Adjust these techniques based on your preferred crust texture, toppings, and oven characteristics for your ideal pizza experience!

Oven Baking Method

1. Preparation
   - Pre-heat your oven to the highest temperature possible, usually around 500°F (260°C), and place a pizza stone or baking sheet inside while preheating.

2. Assembly
   - Prepare your pizza by rolling out the dough, adding sauce, toppings, and cheese according to your preference.

3. Baking

- Carefully transfer the assembled pizza onto the preheated pizza stone or baking sheet.
- Bake the pizza for approximately 10-15 minutes or until the crust is golden brown, the cheese is melted, and the toppings are cooked to your liking.
- Rotate the pizza halfway through the baking process for even cooking.

4. Check for Doneness

- Keep an eye on the pizza as it bakes to avoid burning.
- Adjust the baking time as needed based on your oven's performance and desired level of crispness.

5. Rest and Serve

- Once done, remove the pizza from the oven and let it rest for a few minutes before slicing.
- This allows the cheese to set and prevents toppings from sliding off when sliced.

Grilled Pizza Method

1. Preparation
   - Preheat your grill to medium high heat (around 400-450°F/200-230°C).

2. Preparation of Pizza
   - Roll out your pizza dough and lightly oil one side to prevent sticking on the grill.

3. Grilling the Pizza
   - Place the oiled side of the dough directly onto the grill grates, oiled side down.
   - Grill the dough for 23 minutes or until it starts to bubble and grill marks appear on the bottom.
   - Keep an eye on it to prevent burning.

4. Flipping and Topping
   - Once the bottom is grilled, remove the dough from the grill.
   - Flip the dough so the grilled side is facing up and quickly add your sauce, toppings, and cheese to the grilled side.

5. Return to Grill

- Place the pizza back on the grill, cover, and cook for another 57 minutes or until the crust is cooked through and the cheese is melted.

6. Check and Serve
- Monitor the pizza to avoid burning. Once done, remove it from the grill, let it rest for a minute, slice, and serve.

Additional Tips

- When grilling pizza, it's essential to work quickly after flipping the dough to ensure toppings are added before the crust overcooks.
- Experiment with different toppings and cheese distribution for both oven baked and grilled pizzas to find your preferred flavor profile.

Both oven baked and grilled pizza methods offer distinct flavors and textures. Choose the method that suits your preferences and available equipment for a delightful homemade pizza experience.

Cast Iron Skillet Pizza

1. Preparation
   - Preheat your oven to the highest temperature, usually around 500°F (260°C).
   - Place a cast iron skillet inside while preheating.

2. Dough Preparation
   - Roll out your pizza dough to fit the size of the skillet.

3. Cooking in the Skillet
   - Carefully remove the preheated skillet from the oven and place it on the stovetop over medium high heat.
   - Lightly oil the skillet and carefully transfer the rolled out dough to the hot skillet.

4. Sauce and Toppings
   - Quickly add your sauce, toppings, and cheese to the dough in the skillet.

5. Baking in the Oven
   - Place the skillet with the assembled pizza into the preheated oven.

- Bake for approximately 10-15 minutes or until the crust is golden brown, the cheese is melted, and the toppings are cooked to your liking.

6. Check and Serve

- Keep an eye on the pizza to prevent burning.
- Once done, carefully remove the skillet from the oven, let it cool for a few minutes, slice, and serve.

Wood-Fired Pizza Oven (if available)

1. Preparation

- Preheat your woodfired pizza oven to a high temperature, typically around 700-900°F (370-480°C).
- Ensure the oven is properly heated and the floor is evenly hot.

2. Assemble Pizza

- Prepare your pizza by rolling out the dough and adding sauce, toppings, and cheese according to your preference.

3. Baking in the Oven

- Slide the assembled pizza onto a pizza peel dusted with cornmeal or flour to prevent sticking.
- Quickly transfer the pizza into the wood fired oven, placing it directly on the hot oven floor or on a pizza stone inside the oven.

4. Monitor the Pizza
- Watch the pizza closely as it bakes in the intense heat of the woodfired oven.
- It will cook very quickly, typically in 15 minutes, depending on the oven's temperature.

5. Check and Serve
- Using the pizza peel, carefully remove the finished pizza from the oven, let it rest for a minute, slice, and serve hot.

Additional Tips
- For the cast iron skillet method, ensure your skillet is well seasoned to prevent sticking.
- Wood-fired pizza ovens provide rapid cooking times, so be vigilant to prevent the pizza from burning.

Special Pizza Recipes

Here are a few unique and special pizza recipes to add some flair to your homemade pizza experience:

1. Margherita Pizza with a Twist

Ingredients
- Fresh tomatoes, sliced
- Fresh mozzarella cheese, sliced
- Fresh basil leaves
- Balsamic glaze (reduced balsamic vinegar)

Instructions
- Assemble the pizza with tomato slices and mozzarella. Bake until the cheese melts.
- After baking, top with fresh basil leaves and drizzle with balsamic glaze for added flavor.

2. BBQ Chicken Pizza

Ingredients
- Cooked chicken, shredded or diced
- BBQ sauce
- Red onions, thinly sliced

- Monterey Jack or cheddar cheese
- Cilantro, chopped (optional)

Instructions

- Spread BBQ sauce on the pizza dough.
- Add cooked chicken, sliced onions, and cheese.
- Bake until the cheese is melted and bubbly. Top with chopped cilantro before serving.

3. Mediterranean Veggie Pizza

Ingredients

- Pesto sauce (as base)
- Roasted red peppers, sliced
- Kalamata olives, sliced
- Artichoke hearts, chopped
- Feta cheese, crumbled

Instructions

- Spread pesto on the dough.
- Add roasted red peppers, olives, and artichoke hearts.
- Sprinkle crumbled feta cheese on top.
- Bake until the crust is golden and the cheese melts.

4. Taco Pizza

Ingredients

- Refried beans (as base)
- Ground beef or turkey, cooked with taco seasoning
- Cheddar cheese, shredded
- Lettuce, diced tomatoes, and sour cream (for topping after baking)

Instructions

- Spread a layer of refried beans on the dough.
- Add the cooked taco seasoned meat and shredded cheddar cheese.
- Bake until the cheese melts.
- Top with lettuce, diced tomatoes, and a dollop of sour cream before serving.

5. Breakfast Pizza

Ingredients

- Breakfast sausage or bacon, cooked and crumbled
- Scrambled eggs
- Cheddar cheese or mozzarella
- Sliced green onions or chives (optional)

Instructions

- Spread a layer of scrambled eggs on the pizza dough.

- Add the cooked sausage or bacon and sprinkle cheese on top.
- Bake until the cheese is melted.
- Garnish with sliced green onions or chives before serving.

6. Margherita Pizza

Ingredients
- Pizza dough
- 12 ripe tomatoes, thinly sliced
- Fresh mozzarella cheese, sliced or torn
- Fresh basil leaves
- Olive oil
- Salt and pepper to taste
- Optional: Balsamic glaze

Instructions
- Pre-heat your oven to the highest temperature, usually around 500°F (260°C).
- Roll out the pizza dough to your desired thickness on a floured surface.
- Place the rolled dough on a pizza stone or baking sheet.
- Drizzle olive oil over the dough and spread it evenly.
- Arrange the tomato slices evenly over the dough.

- Add slices or torn pieces of fresh mozzarella on top of the tomatoes.
- Season with salt and pepper to taste.
- Bake in the preheated oven for 10-15 minutes or until the crust is golden and the cheese is melted and bubbly.
- Once baked, remove the pizza from the oven and garnish with fresh basil leaves.
- Optionally, drizzle balsamic glaze over the pizza before serving.

7. Pepperoni Lovers' Delight

Ingredients
- Pizza dough
- Pizza sauce
- Pepperoni slices
- Shredded mozzarella cheese
- Grated Parmesan cheese
- Olive oil
- Dried oregano
- Red pepper flakes (optional)

Instructions
- Pre-heat your oven to 500°F (260°C).

- Roll out the pizza dough and place it on a pizza stone or baking sheet.
- Spread pizza sauce evenly over the dough, leaving a small border for the crust.
- Sprinkle a generous amount of shredded mozzarella cheese over the sauce.
- Place pepperoni slices evenly on top of the cheese.
- Add a sprinkle of grated Parmesan cheese over the pepperoni.
- Drizzle a bit of olive oil over the toppings.
- Sprinkle dried oregano and red pepper flakes (if using) over the pizza for added flavor.
- Bake in the preheated oven for 1015 minutes or until the crust is golden brown and the cheese is melted and bubbly.
- Remove from the oven, let it cool for a minute, slice, and serve hot.

8. Veggie Supreme Pizza

Ingredients

- Pizza dough
- Pizza sauce
- Sliced bell peppers (red, green, yellow)
- Sliced red onions
- Sliced mushrooms
- Sliced black olives
- Cherry tomatoes, halved
- Spinach leaves
- Shredded mozzarella cheese
- Olive oil
- Salt, pepper, and Italian seasoning to taste

Instructions

- Pre-heat your oven to 500°F (260°C).
- Roll out the pizza dough and place it on a pizza stone or baking sheet.
- Spread pizza sauce evenly over the dough, leaving a small border.
- Sprinkle a layer of shredded mozzarella cheese over the sauce.
- Layer sliced bell peppers, red onions, mushrooms, black olives, cherry tomatoes, and spinach leaves on top of the cheese.

- Drizzle a bit of olive oil over the vegetables and season with salt, pepper, and Italian seasoning.
- Bake in the preheated oven for 12-15 minutes or until the crust is golden and the cheese is melted and bubbly.
- Remove from the oven, let it cool for a minute, slice, and serve.

9. Seafood Sensation Pizza

Ingredients

- Pizza dough
- Alfredo sauce or garlic sauce
- Cooked shrimp, peeled and deveined
- Chopped cooked crab or imitation crab meat
- Sliced calamari rings (optional)
- Minced garlic
- Shredded mozzarella cheese
- Grated Parmesan cheese
- Fresh parsley, chopped
- Olive oil
- Salt and pepper to taste

Instructions

- Pre-heat your oven to 500°F (260°C).
- Roll out the pizza dough and place it on a pizza stone or baking sheet.
- Spread Alfredo sauce or garlic sauce evenly over the dough, leaving a small border.
- Sprinkle a layer of shredded mozzarella cheese over the sauce.
- Distribute cooked shrimp, chopped crab meat, and sliced calamari (if using) over the cheese.
- Sprinkle minced garlic over the seafood.

- Drizzle a bit of olive oil over the toppings and season with salt and pepper.
- Top with grated Parmesan cheese and fresh parsley.
- Bake in the preheated oven for 1215 minutes or until the crust is golden and the cheese is melted and bubbly.
- Remove from the oven, let it cool for a minute, slice, and serve.

10. Fruit and Nutella Dessert Pizza

Ingredients
- Pizza dough (sweet dough, if available)
- Nutella or chocolate hazelnut spread
- Sliced strawberries
- Sliced bananas
- Blueberries or raspberries
- Chopped nuts (walnuts, almonds, or hazelnuts)
- Powdered sugar for dusting (optional)
- Whipped cream or vanilla ice cream (optional, for serving)

Instructions
- Pre-heat your oven to 400°F (200°C).
- Roll out the pizza dough on a baking sheet or pizza stone.

- Spread Nutella or chocolate hazelnut spread evenly over the dough.
- Arrange sliced strawberries, bananas, blueberries or raspberries, and chopped nuts on top of the spread.
- Bake in the preheated oven for 1012 minutes or until the crust is golden brown.
- Once baked, remove from the oven and let it cool for a few minutes.
- Optionally, dust the pizza with powdered sugar for added sweetness.
- Slice the dessert pizza and serve with a dollop of whipped cream or a scoop of vanilla ice cream if desired.

11. Cinnamon Sugar Apple Dessert Pizza

Ingredients

- Pizza dough (sweet dough, if available)
- Apple slices (thinly sliced)
- Brown sugar
- Cinnamon powder
- Butter (melted)
- Caramel sauce (optional)
- Vanilla ice cream (optional, for serving)

Instructions

- Pre-heat your oven to 400°F (200°C).
- Roll out the pizza dough on a baking sheet or pizza stone.
- Arrange thinly sliced apples over the dough, covering the entire surface.
- In a small bowl, mix brown sugar and cinnamon powder. Sprinkle the mixture evenly over the apples.
- Drizzle melted butter over the sugar cinnamon apple topping.
- Bake in the preheated oven for 12-15 minutes or until the crust is golden brown and the apples are tender.
- Once baked, remove from the oven and let it cool slightly.

- Optionally, drizzle caramel sauce over the pizza for added sweetness.
- Slice the dessert pizza and serve warm with a scoop of vanilla ice cream on top if desired.

These dessert pizzas offer a delightful way to satisfy your sweet tooth. Customize the toppings and flavors to create your own unique and delicious dessert pizza experience!

Tips and Tricks

Here are some tips and tricks for achieving a perfect pizza crust and getting creative with flavors:

Secrets to a Perfect Crust

1. Use High Heat
Pre-heat your oven or grill to the highest temperature possible. This ensures a crispy crust and quick cooking, preventing a soggy bottom.

2. Quality Ingredients
Use high-quality flour for your dough and fresh yeast for optimal rising. Quality ingredients contribute to a better texture and flavor.

3. Resting the Dough
Allow the pizza dough to rest after shaping it. This allows the gluten to relax, making it easier to shape and preventing the dough from shrinking when baked.

4. Pizza Stone or Baking Steel

Pre-heat a pizza stone or baking steel in the oven before placing the pizza on it. These surfaces help absorb moisture, resulting in a crispier crust.

5. Thinly Rolled Dough

Roll the dough thinly and evenly to achieve a crispy crust. Thicker dough may result in a softer crust.

6. Cornmeal or Semolina Flour

Use cornmeal or semolina flour under the pizza dough before baking to prevent sticking and add extra crispiness to the crust.

Getting Creative with Flavors

1. Homemade Sauces

Experiment with homemade sauces like pesto, white sauce, or BBQ sauce instead of traditional tomato based pizza sauce for unique flavor profiles.

2. Unusual Toppings

Get creative with toppings such as roasted vegetables, caramelized onions, figs, fig jam, arugula, or even sliced apples for a sweet and savory twist.

3. Cheese Varieties

Try different cheese combinations like goat cheese, feta, blue cheese, or smoked gouda to add depth and richness to your pizza.

4. Fresh Herbs and Spices

Use fresh herbs like basil, thyme, or rosemary, and spices like red pepper flakes, garlic powder, or truffle oil to elevate flavors.

5. Sweet and Savory Combos

Experiment with sweet and savory combinations by adding ingredients like honey drizzles, balsamic reductions, or fruits on savory pizzas.

6. Seasonal Ingredients

Utilize seasonal produce for unique flavor profiles and to keep your pizzas fresh and intune with the flavors of the season.

7. Smoked or Grilled Ingredients

Incorporate smoked or grilled elements like smoked meats, grilled vegetables, or even grilled pineapple for added depth and smoky flavors.

Using these tips and exploring creative flavor combinations can take your homemade pizzas to new heights, allowing you to create unique and personalized culinary experiences with every slice!Absolutely! Here's guidance on making pizzas for various dietary restrictions and tips for storing and reheating leftover pizza:

Pizza for Dietary Restrictions

1. GlutenFree Pizza

- Use gluten free pizza dough made from rice flour, almond flour, or a gluten free flour blend.
- Ensure all toppings, sauces, and seasonings are gluten free.
- Opt for fresh ingredients to avoid cross contamination.

2. Dairy-Free Pizza

- Substitute traditional cheese with dairy free alternatives like vegan cheese, cashew cheese, or nutritional yeast for a cheesy flavor.
- Use olive oil, pesto, or tomato based sauces instead of creamy or cheese based sauces.

Vegan Pizza

- Use a vegan-friendly pizza dough recipe or choose a pre-made vegan dough.
- Skip animal based toppings like meat and opt for veggies, tofu, tempeh, or plant based proteins.
- Use vegan cheese or make your own using cashews, nutritional yeast, and seasonings.

Storing and Reheating Pizza

Storing Pizza

- Store leftover pizza in an airtight container or wrap it tightly in plastic wrap and place it in the refrigerator.
- If stacking slices, place parchment paper or foil between them to prevent sticking.

Reheating Pizza

<u>**Oven Method**</u>

1. Preheat your oven to 375°F (190°C).

2. Place the pizza slices on a baking sheet or directly on the oven rack for a crispier crust.

3. Bake for about 10-15 minutes or until heated through and the crust becomes crispy.

Skillet Method

1. Preheat a skillet over medium heat.

2. Place the pizza slice(s) in the skillet and cover it with a lid to trap heat.

3. Cook for 35 minutes or until the bottom is crispy and the toppings are heated.

Microwave Method

1. Place a microwave safe plate in the microwave.

2. Arrange the pizza slices on the plate and cover them with a damp paper towel to prevent moisture loss.

3. Microwave for 30 seconds to 1 minute or until heated through.

Additional Tips

- If reheating in the oven, placing a small cup of water in the oven can help prevent the pizza from drying out.

- For a crispier crust when reheating in the oven, place the pizza directly on the oven rack or use a pizza stone.

By adhering to specific dietary needs and following proper storing and reheating techniques, you can enjoy delicious homemade pizzas even when accommodating dietary restrictions. Adjust recipes and reheating methods as needed to suit individual preferences and dietary needs.

Home-made Pizza Business

Starting a homemade pizza business can be an exciting venture. Here are steps to guide you through setting up your homemade pizza business:

1. Research and Planning

Market Research

- Analyze the local market to understand the demand for homemade pizzas.
- Identify competitors, their offerings, and pricing.
- Determine your target audience and their preferences.

Business Plan

Create a comprehensive business plan outlining your goals, target market, unique selling proposition, menu, pricing strategy, operational plan, and marketing approach.

2. Legal Requirements

Permits and Licenses

Obtain necessary permits and licenses required for a food business in your area. This includes health department permits, food handling certifications, and business operation licenses.

Regulations and Compliance

Ensure compliance with local health and safety regulations, including food preparation standards and sanitation requirements.

3. Kitchen Setup and Supplies

Workspace

Establish a designated cooking area adhering to local health and safety regulations. This can be a commercial kitchen or a separate section of your home kitchen, depending on local laws.

Equipment and Ingredients

Invest in essential equipment such as ovens, prep tables, utensils, and refrigeration. Source high quality ingredients for your pizzas.

4. Menu Development

Menu Offerings

- Create a diverse and appealing menu with various pizza options, catering to different tastes and dietary preferences.
- Experiment with unique toppings, flavors, and sizes to differentiate your offerings.

5. Branding and Marketing

Brand Establishment

Develop a memorable brand identity, including a business name, logo, and brand message that reflects the essence of your homemade pizza business.

Marketing Strategy

- Utilize multiple marketing channels, including social media, a business website, local advertising, and collaborations with local events or businesses.
- Offer promotions, discounts, or loyalty programs to attract and retain customers.

6. Operations and Customer Service

Streamlined Operations

- Establish efficient workflows for order taking, preparation, baking, and delivery or pickup.
- Focus on consistency in taste, quality, and timely delivery of orders.

Customer Experience

Prioritize excellent customer service, listen to customer feedback, and make necessary improvements based on their suggestions.

7. Launch and Growth

Soft Launch and Feedback

Conduct a soft launch to test your operations, gather feedback, and make necessary adjustments before a full scale launch.

Growth Strategies

- Continuously innovate your menu, expand offerings, and seek opportunities for partnerships or collaborations to grow your customer base.
- Consider delivery services, catering for events, or participating in local markets to reach a broader audience.

Starting a homemade pizza business requires thorough planning, adherence to regulations, attention to quality, and effective marketing strategies. With dedication and a passion for making delicious pizzas, you can build a successful homemade pizza brand. Always ensure legal compliance and prioritize customer satisfaction for long term success.

Trouble-shooting and FAQs

Dough Issues

Problem: Dough doesn't rise properly.
Solution: Ensure the yeast is not expired and the water temperature for activating the yeast is between 105-110°F (40-43°C). Allow sufficient time for proofing.

Problem: Dough is too sticky or too dry.
Solution: Adjust flour or water quantities gradually until the dough reaches the desired consistency. Humidity levels can also affect dough texture.

Baking Problems

Problem: Pizza crust is too soggy or undercooked.
Solution: Preheat your oven sufficiently and use a pizza stone or baking steel. Ensure the oven is at the highest temperature possible for a crispier crust.

Problem: Burnt toppings or unevenly cooked pizza.
Solution: Experiment with different topping placements or slice thicknesses. Rotate the pizza halfway through baking to ensure even cooking.

Frequently Asked Questions (FAQs)

1. How do I store leftover pizza?
Store leftover pizza in an air-tight container or wrap it tightly in plastic wrap and refrigerate for up to 34 days.

2. Can I freeze pizza dough?
Yes, you can freeze pizza dough. Portion the dough, wrap it tightly in plastic wrap or place it in a freezer bag, and freeze for up to 3 months. Thaw in the refrigerator overnight before use.

3. How do I reheat pizza without it becoming soggy?
Reheat pizza slices in the oven or toaster oven at 375°F (190°C) on a baking sheet for crispy results. Another method is to reheat in a skillet on the stovetop over medium heat until the crust becomes crispy.

4. What is the best flour for pizza dough?
High protein flours like bread flour or Italian Tipo "00" flour are commonly used for pizza dough as they yield a chewier and crispier crust.

5. How can I speed up the dough rising process?

Place the dough in a warm, draft free area. You can also slightly increase the yeast quantity or use warm (but not hot) water to activate the yeast.

6. Can I make gluten-free or vegan pizza?

Yes, you can make gluten-free pizza using alternative flours like rice flour or almond flour. For vegan pizza, use plant based toppings, dairy free cheese, and ensure no animal products are used in the dough.

7. What are some creative pizza topping ideas?

Get creative with toppings such as caramelized onions, roasted garlic, fresh herbs, figs, arugula, pine nuts, or even truffle oil for unique flavor profiles.

These troubleshooting tips and FAQs can assist in addressing common challenges and provide helpful guidance for successfully navigating various aspects of making homemade pizzas and running a pizza business.

Common Pizza-Making Mistakes

Common pizza-making mistakes and tips to overcome them:

1. Using Cold Dough

<u>Mistake</u>: Using dough straight from the refrigerator can result in a tougher crust and uneven cooking.

<u>Tip</u>: Allow the dough to come to room temperature for about 30-60 minutes before shaping and baking. This helps the dough relax and rise properly.

2. Overloading with Toppings

<u>Mistake</u>: Adding too many toppings can weigh down the pizza, making the crust soggy and preventing even cooking.

<u>Tip</u>: Use a balance of toppings to avoid overwhelming the pizza. Opt for fewer toppings or spread them evenly for better results.

3. Incorrect Oven Temperature

<u>Mistake</u>: Baking at the wrong temperature can lead to undercooked or burnt pizzas.

<u>Tip</u>: Preheat your oven adequately. High temperatures (around 500°F/260°C) help achieve a crispier crust. Use a pizza stone or baking steel for even heat distribution.

4. Using Too Much Sauce

<u>Mistake</u>: Applying too much sauce can make the pizza soggy and overpower the flavors of other ingredients.

Tip: Use a moderate amount of sauce and spread it evenly, leaving a thin layer to prevent the crust from becoming soggy.

5. Not Preheating the Pizza Stone or Baking Surface
Mistake: Placing the pizza on a cold baking surface results in an unevenly cooked crust.
Tip: Always preheat the pizza stone or baking sheet in the oven before placing the pizza on it. This ensures a crispy bottom crust.

6. Ignoring the Resting Time
Mistake: Not allowing the dough to rest before baking can cause the pizza to shrink or result in a tough crust.
Tip: After shaping the dough, let it rest for about 1015 minutes to relax the gluten before adding toppings and baking.

7. Using LowQuality Ingredients:
Mistake: Using low quality or overly processed ingredients can impact the overall taste and quality of the pizza.
Tip: Opt for fresh and high quality ingredients. Fresh vegetables, good quality cheese, and flavorful sauces elevate the taste of homemade pizzas.

8. Cutting Pizza Immediately After Baking

<u>Mistake</u>: Cutting into the pizza right after baking can cause the toppings to slide off and the cheese to run.

<u>Tip</u>: Allow the pizza to rest for a few minutes after baking to let the cheese settle before cutting. This helps retain the toppings and flavors.

Avoiding these common pizzamaking mistakes can significantly improve the quality and taste of your homemade pizzas, ensuring a more enjoyable culinary experience!

Frequently Asked Questions (FAQs) about pizza making along with quick solutions:

1. FAQ: My pizza crust is too thick. How do I make it thinner?

Quick Solution: Roll out the dough more thinly. Use a rolling pin or your hands to stretch and flatten the dough further. Work from the center outwards to achieve an even thickness.

2. FAQ: My pizza crust is too thin and tears easily. What can I do?

Quick Solution: Allow the dough to rest after shaping to relax the gluten. Use a gentle touch when stretching the dough. If it tears, patch it together gently, or reshape it slightly.

3. FAQ: My pizza crust is not crispy enough. How can I achieve a crispier crust?

Quick Solution: Ensure the oven is properly preheated to the highest temperature. Use a pizza stone or baking steel to bake the pizza. Also, avoid overloading the pizza with toppings, as excess moisture can prevent a crispy crust.

4. FAQ: How do I prevent a soggy pizza bottom?

Quick Solution: Preheat the oven with the pizza stone or baking sheet inside. Ensure the dough is not too thick and use a moderate amount of sauce to prevent excess moisture. Sprinkle cornmeal or semolina on the baking surface to absorb moisture and prevent sticking.

5. FAQ: My pizza toppings are not cooking evenly. What should I do?

Quick Solution: Ensure the toppings are cut uniformly and not too thick. Distribute them evenly across the pizza. Consider partially cooking certain ingredients like thicker vegetables before placing them on the pizza.

6. FAQ: My pizza is burnt on the edges but undercooked in the center. How can I avoid this?

Quick Solution: Adjust the oven rack to a lower position to prevent the top from burning while the center cooks. Alternatively, reduce the oven temperature slightly and extend the baking time for a more evenly cooked pizza.

7. FAQ: How can I prevent the cheese from burning?

Quick Solution: Use high quality cheese that melts evenly. Consider using a blend of cheeses, including low moisture mozzarella, to prevent excessive browning. Cover the pizza with foil halfway through baking to protect the cheese from burning.

8. FAQ: Can I make pizza dough in advance and freeze it?

Quick Solution: Yes, you can freeze pizza dough. Portion it, wrap it tightly in plastic wrap or place it in a freezer bag, and freeze for up to three months. Thaw it overnight in the refrigerator before using.

These quick solutions address common concerns when making homemade pizzas, offering fast remedies to improve your pizza-making experience.

Conclusion

Creating delicious homemade pizzas can be an immensely rewarding experience, whether you're an enthusiast exploring new flavors or considering turning this passion into a business. By mastering the art of pizzamaking and understanding the nuances involved, you can craft flavorful, crispy, and visually appealing pizzas right in your own kitchen.

From exploring the basics of pizza preparation to delving into the history, dough making techniques, sauce variations, diverse toppings, and various cooking methods, this guide has aimed to equip you with the knowledge and tips needed to elevate your pizza-making game.

Remember, perfecting the craft takes practice, patience, and a willingness to experiment. Embrace your creativity by exploring different combinations of toppings, experimenting with unique flavors, and adapting recipes to suit dietary preferences or business ventures.

Whether you're making pizzas for your family, friends, or considering starting a homemade pizza business, paying attention to quality ingredients, proper techniques, and customer satisfaction will set you on the path to success.

Now, armed with troubleshooting insights, FAQs, and quick solutions to common challenges, you're better equipped to troubleshoot issues that may arise while preparing your pizzas, ensuring your pizza-making journey is as enjoyable and delicious as possible.

So, roll out that dough, unleash your culinary creativity, and savor the joy of crafting exceptional homemade pizzas! Cheers to your continued success in the world of pizza-making.

Appendix: Pizza Recipes Index

This index provides a quick reference guide to the various pizza recipes featured throughout the book, allowing readers to easily navigate and locate their preferred pizza recipes in the main content.

Classic Pizza Recipes
1. Margherita Pizza
A traditional Italian pizza featuring tomatoes, mozzarella, basil, and olive oil.

2. Pepperoni Lovers' Delight
Loaded with pepperoni slices, mozzarella cheese, and a tangy tomato sauce.

Specialty Pizzas
3. Veggie Supreme
A colorful combination of bell peppers, onions, mushrooms, olives, tomatoes, and spinach.

4. Seafood Sensation
Featuring shrimp, crab, calamari, and a blend of Alfredo or garlic sauce.

Dessert Pizzas:

5. Fruit and Nutella Dessert Pizza

Topped with Nutella, strawberries, bananas, blueberries, and nuts.

6. Cinnamon Sugar Apple Dessert Pizza

Layered with apple slices, brown sugar, cinnamon, and drizzled with caramel.

Gluten-Free and Vegan Options:

7. Gluten-Free Pizza Dough

A gluten free alternative using rice or almond flour for the dough.

8. Vegan Pizza

Incorporating plant based toppings and dairy free cheese for a vegan friendly option.

Unique and Creative Combinations

9. BBQ Chicken

A twist with BBQ sauce, grilled chicken, red onions, and cilantro.

10. Mediterranean Delight

Featuring sundried tomatoes, feta cheese, Kalamata olives, and fresh oregano.

Note

Detailed recipes for each pizza type can be found in the respective sections within the main content of this book.

Appendix: Ingredient Measurement Conversion Tables

Volume Conversions

1 teaspoon (tsp) = 5 milliliters (ml)

1 tablespoon (Tbsp) = 15 milliliters (ml)

1 fluid ounce (fl oz) = 30 milliliters (ml)

1 cup = 240 milliliters (ml)

1 pint = 473 milliliters (ml)

1 quart = 946 milliliters (ml)

1 gallon = 3.785 liters (l)

Weight Conversions

1 ounce (oz) = 28.35 grams (g)

1 pound (lb) = 453.59 grams (g)

1 kilogram (kg) = 2.205 pounds (lb)

Oven Temperature Conversions

Celsius to Fahrenheit: °C x 9/5 + 32 = °F

Fahrenheit to Celsius: (°F 32) x 5/9 = °C

This format includes convenient tables for volume, weight, and oven temperature conversions, aiding readers in converting measurements for ingredients and temperatures as needed.

About The Author

Christabel Henry is a nutritionist, who is keen on personal development and very interested in the wellness and well-being of everyone. In a cozy corner filled with nutrition-packed snacks, the passionate nutritionist meticulously crafts her latest masterpiece—a comprehensive book that unravels the intricate tapestry of health and nourishment. With every keystroke, she weaves together a symphony of science-backed information, practical tips, and delectable recipes, aiming to empower readers with the knowledge to make informed dietary choices. As the chapters take shape, her words inspire a journey towards a balanced and vibrant life, creating a guide that will illuminate the path to wellness for countless eager readers.

www.ingramcontent.com/pod-product-compliance
Lightning Source LLC
Chambersburg PA
CBHW062325290526
45794CB00005B/1900

* 9 7 9 8 8 7 2 1 6 7 4 1 9 *